MY BOOK OF THE LORD'S PRAYER

MY

BOOK OF THE LORD'S PRAYER

by Eileen Lomasney, CSJ   art by Alice Hausner

CONCORDIA®

Publishing House
St. Louis   London

to my Mother and Father

Library of Congress Cataloging in Publication Data

Lomasney, Eileen.
    My book of the Lord's prayer.

    Includes text of the Lord's prayer.
    1. Lord's prayer—Juvenile literature. I. Lord's prayer.
English. 1976. II. Title.
BV232.L58   226′.96′07   76-2707
ISBN 0-570-03456-6

Concordia Publishing House, St. Louis, Missouri
Copyright © 1976 by Concordia Publishing House

Manufactured in the United States of America

JESUS TEACHES US ABOUT PRAYER*

One day a friend asked Jesus
To teach us how to pray,
And Jesus did—then gave us all
A perfect prayer to say.

"You don't need many words," He said,
"Because your Father knows
Your needs before you even ask
(And more than you suppose!).

"Your prayer need not be long nor hard,
For God to hear you pray;
Just talk to Him with loving heart—
And *mean* the words you say!"

*(From Matthew 6:7-9)

OUR FATHER ...

Though God set life upon its course
And made the world come true,
He is *your* Father, and He holds
A Father's love for you.

And so, though He is Lord of all
In earth and sea and sky,
The good news *is* that *you* are quite
The apple of His eye!

... WHO ART IN HEAVEN,

Do you know where heaven is?
Is it near, or far?
It's nearer than your heartbeat,
Yet past the farthest star.

It's everywhere God's love is—
And where His children share
His love with one another,
It is *especially* there.

So when you say, "Our Father
Who art in heaven," *do*
Remember you're in heaven—
For *He* is here with you!

HALLOWED BE THY NAME;

Your name is very beautiful
Because it stands for *you*,
And those who know and love you well
Will tell you this is true.

We treasure every syllable
Of names we speak with love—
But God's is far more wonderful
Than we've a notion of.

And so we keep it holy:
We say it like a prayer,
So when His children call Him,
He will be present there!

THY KINGDOM COME;

We pray to have God's Kingdom come—
For when it does, *all* men
Will live in peace, in love, and joy
As brothers do or friends.

That day will be most wonderful.
Yet where God's law shines clear
In hearts that love Him, Jesus said,
It is already here!

THY WILL BE DONE ON EARTH

AS IT IS IN HEAVEN;

God's will on earth is heaven's law,
And heaven's law is love;
The same love Jesus truly lived
And often told us of.

"Love God," He said, "with all your heart
And others as yourself."
But oh, you cannot keep this law
In books upon a shelf.

You keep it when you try to live
(As I am *sure* you do)
Each day with love and gentleness:
For that's God's will for you!

GIVE US THIS DAY

OUR DAILY BREAD;

It sometimes happens that we fret
For unimportant things:
We tease for some new racing car
Or for a doll that sings.

But Jesus would remind us, first,
To pray that *no* one know
A need for bread that gives us life
Or food that helps us grow.

It just may happen you've enough
And that you gladly share—
Then you are really helping God
To answer someone's prayer!

AND FORGIVE US OUR TRESPASSES,
AS WE FORGIVE THOSE
WHO TRESPASS AGAINST US;

God knows how miserable we feel
When we've done something wrong;
He takes our sorrow with our love
And gives us back—a song.

Our friends may hurt us, too, at times.
Don't hold a grudge or fuss,
For God expects that we'll forgive—
As He's forgiven us!

AND LEAD US NOT INTO TEMPTATION;

Plants, and animals, and birds,
Fish, and stars, and rocks
Follow out God's law for them
As faithfully as clocks.

But *we* are human: *we* are free!
We choose the way we live.
We're free to *think*, and *be*, and *do:*
To give or not to give.

God asks our love. We ask His help
In every choice we make,
So what we choose will be His will—
And *not a big* mistake!

BUT DELIVER US FROM EVIL;

Cold and sickness, hunger, want—
Are difficult to bear;
We pray for those who suffer them,
And help—because we care.

But pride, and selfishness, and greed
(In a hidden way)
Rob us of our humanness
And eat our joy away.

Sin is the evil we should fear;
Oh, may God keep us free and clear!

FOR THINE IS THE KINGDOM
AND THE POWER
AND THE GLORY FOREVER AND EVER
AMEN.

And so we end our prayer with praise
For God our Father's care,
Because His *kingdom* is our home—
And love shall greet us there.

And for the *power* He alone
Holds over life and death,
We praise Him (and we thank Him, too)
With our smallest breath.

And for His *glory* we give praise
And will forever, when
With Jesus we are safe at home
World without end. Amen!